# GEODE OF OPUS

## THE WHISPER OF HEART

KRISHA K

# Contents

# Contents

# Preface

Sentences finely tuned to give you a beautiful aroma of inked words. Poetry has awakened people's emotions time immemorial. Starting from Walter Whitman who brought a transition between transcendentalism and realism to our famous poets Dr.Rabindranath Tagore, Dr. Sarojini Naidu who fought for our country's freedom through the power of words. The great Mahakavi Subramania Bharathiyar, a freedom fighter, a social reformer who is ever remembered for his poetry which sewed strong emotions in minds of tamil people. Words have been and are potent pills in lighting the inside of us. It changes one's life, steals people's hearts, refreshes and awakens the soundless soul. Moreover, it adds more aesthetic beauty to our lives. Here I present to you my second book "Geode of opus". A small book that is created from my melody of life.

'Geode'- 'Rock of crystals'

'Opus'- 'sets of composition'

"Geode of opus" refers to "treasure of compositions". Poems and one liners written with sweetness of dynamic adventures of life.

Hope you all enjoy the book!

"Poetry is when an emotion has found its thought and the thought has found words"

-Robert frost

*A man is made by his belief. As he believes, so he is.*

*~Bhagavat Gita: chapter 17; verse 3.*

# 1. STAY CHIRPY

*Open the doors of your heart,*

*Breathe the air, thank the universe;*

*Small steps daily towards success*

*Can fetch you oscars*

*Let difficulties be your stepping stone,*

*There is nothing called never*

*Everyday is a new beginning*

*Start it with a graceful humming,*

*An evidence you are improving*

*Is when you start working*

*And*

*Good days are on the way*

*Good people are yet more to meet,*

*Good news are plenty to tweet*

*So embrace yourself*

*And live your life to the fullest*

*For your life shall be fabulous!*

# 2. MOTHER NATURE

*As the rain pours from the sky*

*Clattering on the roof as a diamond's disguise*

*Sky grinned with its flashes of lightning*

*Flowers jewelled with shiny dew drops*

*Fruits hanging as crystals*

*Pecked by the colourful feathery birds*

*As an earthly scent replenishes the land*

*With odes of nature's nourishment*

*Earthlings grow on the lap of mother nature*

*With lullaby of love, with finest care of nature*

*Creations tweet the joy and beauty of this earth!*

# 3. DREAMS AND DESTINY

*I chase my dreams*

*With a scarlet eyes*

*I sacrifice my life*

*For an unknown destiny*

*Yet with a known dream*

*I'm simply supersaturated*

*Yet I'm benevolent*

*For it is worth it to live*

*I rarely remorse*

*For I am a recluse*

*I grow decisive day by day*

*I grow stronger step by step*

*I find myself line by line*

*I'm on my path for a better 'me'*

*But when once I'm done*

*Serving the society*

*Would be my promising priority*

*With a greatful heart*

*And with a gentle smile*

*I shall burn myself to lit up the world*

*To build a reasonable repair*

*Before i take a radiant leave*

*I shall feel the beauty of heal!*

# 4. CALM AND CLASSY

*Cemented heart*

*Feels no pain*

*Knows no anger*

*Still sings the beauty of life*

*Still feels the beauty of love*

# 5. FRIENDSHIP GOALS

*A long drive with my bestie*

*Happiest memories bestowed*

*Embraced the earth's greenery*

*As footsteps unite*

*We walk by the river*

*Redefining love with deep talks*

*Vibrant heart, a mellow mood;*

*Relishing flavours of indian cuisine*

*Happily together we dine*

*At once everything seems fine*

*For talks cured the fever of longingness*

*And the heart blushes in the beauty of pure bonds*

# 6. THANK YOU HARD TIMES!

*Through the journey of life, a special*

*note of thanks to the hard times i faced;*

*You snitched my shyness and timidity*

*and made me extra bold, confident,*

*strong yet flexible and gentle,*

*You became the founder of my clarity!*

# 7. LET ME!

*Let my dreams not let me sleep*

*Let my skin know what sweat is,*

*Let my heart beat with some purpose*

*Let my brain know to work smart*

*Let my soul know what achievement is*

*Let me work for my success*

*Let me have a chance to serve the needy*

*Let me bring change in people's life*

*Let me bring smile in innocent faces*

*Only then this soul shall cease*

*Or never shall I rest in peace!*

# 8. JUST A HAPPY ME!

*As the moist breeze fizzles out*

*My wavy hair waves by the wind*

*As the sun shines*

*My eyes sparkling*

*I perch under the bowers*

*With a hearty smile on my red lips*

*An ecstatic calmness brims my soul*

*I need no prosecco*

*For I am a fantastico*

*And a moulded magnifico!*

# 9. DILIGENCE

*With wounds of pain*

*With scars of failure*

*With one million trials*

*With thousand sacrifices*

*With tears hidden*

*With starvation for success*

*Your dream gets paid*

*For the efforts you made*

*For victory had never been that easy*

*When it pays to be a bit gutsy!*

# 10. SENSITIVE OR SENSIBLE

*From being sensitive to life*

*To being sensitive only for sensible deeds,*

*Life had its tint of blooming maturity*

*And now heart feels light*

*For the emotions had its right!*

# 11. THOUGHTS

*And when my heart beats flutter with happiness*

*Is it your love that keeps my happiness on*

*Or is it my thought that comprehend you!*

# 12. JOY OF VICTORY

*Eyes sparkling with victory*

*Her silent screams stolen off*

*Stolen by her resilient moves of wisdom*

*Sleepless nights with dreams on*

*And that was an extra mile she won*

*And now she stands on the stage*

*With a glow of winning her dreams*

*As thunder of applause radiated her spine*

*Her efforts paid a radiant shine*

*Shine rouse up with one thousand scars*

*For behind the fame there must be a scar*

*A scar that unfolds the beauty of efforts*

*And efforts reveal the clarity of fame!*

# 13. TUNE UP

*When you had a binge suffering*

*That's where your style changes*

*You just grow stronger than your regrets*

*And soon your fruitful emotions*

*work only after your permission*

*And that's off course a great transition!*

# 14. FREELANCE LIFE

*River flowing crystal clear*

*I see my reflections scatter*

*I felt the whole me*

*Being real feels free*

*Accepting my oddity*

*Correcting my flaws*

*Celebrating my nature*

*Makes me feel mature*

*With a glimpsy smile*

*My eyes sparkle*

*And my hair curls sun kissed*

*I stay as my life's freelancer*

*For you never live your life twice*

*So enjoy being a bit wise!*

# 15. THE NIGHT SKY ALLURANCE

*Star shimmering bright*

*Moon with its glowing light*

*Showering its love from a distant gaze*

*Sudden radiance of a shooting star*

*Passed within seconds of spark*

*I closed my eyes tight and prayed*

*To shine bright and reach heights*

*And to serve this world with all my might*

*And there shall I regain my beauty of sight!*

# 16. MERA INDIA

*Tricolour flag holding high*

*With victory our hearts overflow*

*Ours is the land of indivisibility*

*Where people travel with the art of unity*

*Ours is the land of prosperity*

*Where nature's mercy is at bounty*

*With strength to change the world*

*We march towards the power of wisdom*

*The strength of our nation blooms*

*When knowledge plays the power of clarity*

*Where the moral life is mended for ages*

*Our country glows with the value of authenticity.*

# 17. SHE

*She is not just a scripture of beauty*

*But she is the art of life*

*She is not just a scripture of sacrifice*

*But she is the power of clarity*

*She is not just as beautiful as a flower*

*But she is the agony lit to brighten this world*

*She is the spark of immense power*

*She is the light of knowledge*

*She is the power destined to this globe*

*For a better world nourished with love!*

# 18. THE ANKLET STORY

*He worked for day and nights, it was his first small salary. With his soulful heart, he bought anklets rimmed with pearls and bent before his love; then graciously took her feet and strapped the anklets around her ankle with his eyes filled with the grace of love. Nevertheless with her heart overwhelmed, she felt like a queen wearing those pearl braided dazzling anklets.*

*Too much, you say? But human relationships*

*are made valuable this way, I say!*

# 19. PRIORITY

*And...*

*When you closely watch the life of highly successful people,*

*You see they prioritise their work first and other*

*things are left secondary to their dreams*

*They partially detach from things that make them*

*feel sweet and comfortable, for real achievement*

*needs sweat and a fire zone!*

# 20. IT'S FOR YOU!

*You beautiful soul, I'm absolutely proud of you! You rose from where you fell, though things aren't as easy as before; you look happier than your past. You take in efforts to bring out the best version in you and your evolution feels beautiful.*

# 21. SHINE

*Her inner self shimmered with shine*

*She embraced her flaws*

*She stood by the beauty of her dreams*

*She found herself much sweeter than before*

*And a bit wilder than yesterday!*

# 22. ZEALOUS

*Glowing with shades of oddities*

*Fluttering with fire of wisdom*

*Finding happiness in tiny little steps*

*Tiny steps to reach my dreams*

*Chiseled carefully with the beauty of zeal*

*With great efforts, dreams never spared;*

*For it feels better to be dead*

*Than living a lost life instead!*

# 23. ONE LINER

*"A scarred soul shines better,*

*just like the chiselled rocks worshipped*

*for its stature"*

*(Whenever you are in a hard situation of life, remember life is moulding you to a better version and your vicinity towards life enhances. So embrace the process of being chiseled by hardships of life.)*

# 24. CHILDHOOD MEMORIES

*A panoroma of moments,*

*Glistening in the paradise*

*In the deepest hue of memories,*

*Memories that made meaningful stories*

*Stories that had beautiful endings;*

*School life moments...*

*A bliss of beautiful momories*

*Innocent faces, forgetful regrets;*

*Where hearts knew no hatred*

*Our childhood was mastered*

*In the purity of innocent hearts*

*"Innocent hearts that remained connected*

*on the grounds of blissful love"*

# 25. GLANCE

*A moment of glance 2020-2021*

*Surviving far from regular times,*

*Breaching the wounds of heart*

*Facing the odds of life,*

*With odes of faith and hope*

*Scars turned to strength*

*Faded dreams turned into fire*

*Fire that lit a new view to life*

*Quenching the lost chances*

*Burying the past regrets*

*By marking a new beginning*

*"Adding new vibes to life*

*By finding new reasons to live"*

# 26. RARE VIBES

*When a person have you as their biggest treasure*

*When they admire your true nature*

*Be happy with what you are;*

*Accepting your flaws and appreciating your tiny*

*little steps, even hell turns into heaven*

*when you vibe with such people!*

*( You are so lucky to have such precious souls in your life. Always be thankful for such souls.)*

# 27. YOUTH'S REALITY

*Relishing dine inn at comfy refreshment stands, long rides, amusement parks, resorts, cosy parlours to groom themselves, weekly dj's for a feel good mood;*

*To...*

*Part time workers to run their daily chores, eyes filled with burden of what future holds, working their best with zero free time;*

*I could see two extremes of youth,*

*Why do these differences ever exist?*

*Where the former are confused of what to enjoy*

*and where to spend, while the latter suffer to live a*

*regular life. Law of karma felt unfair when I saw these differences.*

# 28. 100 SHADES OF MINE

*I stand before the mirror*

*100 shades of mine*

*Reflections shine*

*I'm the adorer of love*

*I'm the anger of pain*

*I'm the fortune of fame*

*I'm the faller for smile*

*I'm silent for idiocy*

*I'm resilient for evil*

*I'm the ruler for rude*

*So don't try judging me,*

*For you will end up tangled*

*In the hundred shades of mine!*

# 29. ALLURE

*His hands held her hand tight*

*As their glowing eyes looked each other*

*With warmful smile brimming with happiness*

*Their faces shimmered with cute blushes blossoming.*

# 30. SPREAD LOVE

*In this world of hurry*

*Where people learn living lonely*

*Show them how much you care,*

*Share your love and spread positivity*

*Loving and caring yourself is easy,*

*But by sharing and caring for the souls around you*

*You bring happiness into their lives*

*And you make your life worthy to live*

*Be it human or an animal;*

*Make their tiny little world feel special*

*By adding sparkles with your presence*

*Your life feels brimmed up in joy of giving*

*And you'll find your happy reasons for living!*

# 31. REFORM

*The moment I came to know that I was*

*a 'just' person in the crowd;*

*I changed my very style of life that wherever*

*I move now, the whole crowd recognizes my*

*presence as a profit!*

# 32. CHOICE

*In this society,*

*Whether you want to be treated like a charm kid? (or)*

*Whether you want to be treated like a sweety pie? (or)*

*Whether you want to be treated like a hotty one? (or)*

*Whether you want to be treated like a respectful leader?*

*The choice is yours!*

# 33. STRENGTH FROM FAILURE

*It's not the success that holds you high*

*But it's the list of failures that make you strong*

*You learn far better at your hard times*

*Than you learn at your cloud nine!*

# 34. RISE

*Hurt??*

*A better me rose up*

*Failed??*

*A better me rose up*

*Broken??*

*A better me rose up*

*Betrayed??*

*A better me rose up*

*Lost??*

*A better me rose up*

*Scarred??*

*A better me rose up*

*A strong version of mine built up this way,*

*Never was I frightened of hardships I faced*

*I fought for what I am today,*

*"And will fight for the bestest*

*sparkling version of mine for a better morrow!"*

# 35. THE GLOWING SPHERE

*Shining from the distant sky*

*Burning your energy for lives on earth*

*You make us warm, you give us food;*

*You are the fire burning for others cause;*

*You are the lamp built forever*

*Without you oh! brightful sun*

*Life on this planet would just be an unknown dream!*

9 798887 041391

Printed by Libri Plureos GmbH in Hamburg, Germany